MERIDIAN

MERIDIAN

Julie Sumner

Wildhouse
Poetry

Design by Cambridge Creative Group

Published by Wildhouse Poetry, an imprint of Wildhouse Publishing
(www.wildhousepublishing.com). No part of this book may be
reproduced in any manner without the written permission from the
publisher, except in brief quotations embodied in critical articles or
reviews. Contact info@wildhousepublications.com for all requests.

Printed in the USA

ISBN 978-1-961741-09-6

For Eric

Meridian by Julie Sumner is the winner of the inaugural **Wildhouse Poetry Chapbook Contest**, con/verge/nces. The contest was launched in 2023 and judged by award-winning poet and essayist Jane Hirshfield. Ms. Hirshfield's writing and life-work exemplify the central conviction guiding Wildhouse Poetry, which publishes poetry that explores our connectedness within the wider fabric of life and our attentiveness to furthering the integrity of creation. We seek writers who engage readers' imagination and encourage them to find transformative ways of seeing and experiencing life in the midst of the challenges and complexities facing us in these times. We look for poems with a clear and recognizable voice, one rooted in reality and carried by the natural music of language.

Contents

Acknowledgements. vii

Hum 1

Binary Codes. 2

Ultima Thule 3

Evensong. 4

The Glassblower 5

The Babylon Willow 6

Bitter. 7

Broken Ground. 8

Patron Saint of Lost Things. 9

Via Negativa 10

I Love How 11

Handwritten 12

The Final Round 13

Girl Child 14

Embryo Adoption 16

Abide 17

The Things We Ask 19

Chimera 20

Meridian. 21

Birdwatching in Quarantine 22

Grackle. 23

Hawaiian Monk Seal. 24

Bittersweet Vine. 25

Neglected Serapias 26

Found Coin 27

Acknowledgements

Grateful acknowledgment is made to the following publications in which these poems first appeared:

Catalpa: "Grackle" and "Handwritten"

The Cresset: "Hum"

Fathom Magazine: "Birdwatching in Quarantine" and "Meridian"

Intima: A Journal of Narrative Medicine: "The Things We Ask"

Relief: "Abide;" "*Via Negativa*"

Writing the Land: Foodways and Social Justice 2022 Anthology: "Broken Ground"

Hum

You can only hear it in silence—
a low rumble, barely perceptible.

You may initially attribute it
to the refrigerator.

Later, a diesel truck thrumming
down the monochrome highway.

Then, you think it's a seaplane
buzzing down in the bay.

It is none of these.
You turn your head—it's gone.
You hold your breath—it's gone.

You soon suspect the earth itself,
whispering its urgent secrets
to anyone who'll listen:

this is the sound of worms turning,
this is the sound of spider webs unspooling,
this is the sound of gravity folding

    and re-folding the ocean like a garment.

Binary Codes

"Black or white" assumes no responsibility.
It ignores the possibility
of that fringed metamorphosis
from blue to gray to white that washes
over the blue heron's feathers, flown
and ruffling in the breeze blown in from the gulf.

"Left or right" exacts a certain toll,
is ill-equipped to map the root-strewn roll
of the old Cherokee road that dog-legs
just to embrace the creek bottom, then
swerves up the shale-cropped incline
as it climbs cloudward past the tree line.

Ultima Thule

The long winter light drops lines
of shadows across the pavement
straight as blue-ruled notebook paper.

Still blank with possibility,
the morning hovers with vast polar hours
stretching out before the horizon.

Time becomes a trick of light, a mirage
of possibility, and I, like the grizzle-bearded
Arctic surveyors, am deceived,

seeing a vast land before me, ripe for plundering,
instead of the truth of the empty line
of ocean meeting sky.

This morning with its vast polar hours,
and the notebook blank before me.
And there will never be more time.

Evensong

It is October.
Outside the kitchen window, the sky flares
into sunset early, unable to contain
the pinkness of itself before nightfall.

The television murmurs its tragedies
in the next room, pitch rising and falling
with produced intent. The glow
from the impalpable pixels casts
a blue hue through the doorway,
somehow too bright for any kind of lament.

Here in the kitchen,
the story's more a silent song.
The lacquered hide of the eggplant
conceals its pale, green flesh;
sun, wind, and water are sewn
in the stories of its seeds.

As my fingertips
trace this vegetable braille,
I find rumors of photons
unfolding each greening leaf,
and read elegies written for all
of those blackened and burned
in the late Easter freeze.

The Glassblower

In the midst of the kitsch of the county craft fair
filled with crocheted baby blankets and velvet Elvis portraits,

the glass blower adjusts his shoulders and sweat weaves
a spine-shaped shadow down the back of his shirt.

His whole body contracts as he exhales.
His breath is a bridled wave flowing through the blow pipe.

The molten orange glass stretches like a belly
with a baby in its womb, and wobbles under its girth.

We hold our breath as we watch him spin the burning glass
into shape, the flames of his crucible engulfing our peripheral vision.

A crowd has gathered with us, fire always drawing
things to itself. The glassblower is a showman now.

He waves the cooling glass globe close to us, certain
of his success in such a delicate and dangerous endeavor.

He clips it free, presenting his masterpiece in blue and green,
the very earth itself, suspended before us, one great breath held within.

The Babylon Willow

Every tree that weeps
is a hybrid of our own hands,
grafted to grow
into the softened shape
of our sorrow.

Even the diamond light
cannot straighten these limbs
bowed under the burden
of our parabolic hurt. Each one
a penitent, licking the earth.

Bitter

—Ruth 1:20-21

Because a life filled with lament can swallow
a person whole, Naomi chose it as a name, Mara,
bitter down through the marrow and bone.

Because there is such a thing as too sweet,
the taste of honey on a molar's exposed nerve
can sear like lightning, cracking bone and teeth.

Because the taste of vinegar can bite,
excoriate your tongue, contract your mouth,
the acid burn a fleeting touch of fire.

Because we can't deny what is within:
we go on living long after we've given in.

Broken Ground

Backbreaking the spring,
rows of seedlings, sewn one
after the other and the other,
straight lines gathering earth
like pleats on a woman's skirt.

Heartbreaking the way the soft,
warm air draws the sap upward
through the greening leaves
of the young spinach just as it does
for the horseweed, the creeping thistle.

Patron Saint of Lost Things

Finding some lost thing
is a paradise all its own.
When that leather wallet
worn smooth as a burro's back
ambles shyly into its old pocket,
or when those Manilow tickets
pry their way from beneath
the fridge like convicts
tunneling out of Sing Sing,
or when those car keys rear
their serrated heads like zombies
emerging from their tomb
of last year's tax returns,
or when that plain wedding band
rolls in shining and leaps back
onto its rightful ring finger,
the kingdom of heaven itself
seems almost at hand.

Via Negativa

Your absence is slowly fashioning
itself two sinewy arms to enclose me,
re-membering itself day by day.

The gap in the kitchen left
by your book-bent head above the table
now ushers in the morning, sun free to fall

over the shadowless oak-grained surface,
the space you lived in, moved in, and breathed in,
now awake, from dust motes weaving a skin,

cobbling odd bones from empty doorframes
and silent thresholds, sculpting muscles
from the smooth, unused side of the bed,

and even hammering together
a heart, it seems, from that persistent tick
of the pendulum clock down the hall.

I Love How

In the West,
the earth fashions itself arms,
complete with angled elbows
and cords of tendons,
reaching upward with rocky hands
toward the blue-shouldered sky
as if it were someone beloved
leaving for good.

Handwritten

Write the word
        light—
see how your thumb
and index finger wave
as flashes on the surface
of moving water,
muscles, ligaments,
tendons bobbing
as the *i* is dotted,
the *t* is crossed,
and somewhere
in the forest of nerves,
that one particular
strike of lightning
spiders across
your interior night,
shining through
every particle
of your own
shadowed body.

The Final Round

She told me it hurt
to raise her left arm,
so much so that just
watering her baskets
of hanging flowers
made her feel like
she'd gone a few rounds
with Mohammed Ali.
She wondered if I could fix it,
massage away this pain.
She said it got worse
when it rained, remembered
it was about the time
of her father's funeral
when it first began.

As my thumb rode
the iron rail of her left triceps,
it fought back gamely,
twitching and dodging,
feinting and bouncing back
as if it had lived life waiting
for the next blow.
And when it didn't come,
as the pad of my thumb
hovered over this
striated fight in her muscle,
the old fear finally gave way
like a towel thrown into the ring,
her whole body lengthening
into the peace of defeat.

Girl Child

"Ten thousand years ago, a group of hunter-gatherers buried an infant girl in an Italian cave with a rich selection of their treasured beads and pendants, showing that even the youngest females were recognized as full persons in their society."

—ScienceDaily (December 14, 2021)

The fossil of you was found
like a shard of sand dollar
trapped in an eon of sand,

a jagged signpost that gestured
toward the small, undiscovered
country of your only life.

Were you the one who smiled
early, passed from knee to knee
around the fire, the first-born child

of the patient daughter, the pink
talisman for better hunting
next moon? Did you clutch and cling

on the shell-smooth beads worn
first by your clan, now your own,
adorned as you were, to enter

the unknown? Many things here
have changed: the world grows warmer,
the world has grown louder, the world

groans. But our language for losing
a child is still ashes, and our word
for *grief* comes from the same word

as *gravid,* each something to be borne.

Embryo Adoption

Where was your soul, love,
those years that you were held
embryonic yet whole, the overflow
of a generous pair of others,

waiting ice-bound and unknown?
Did it hover near the ceiling
like a breath suspended in the cold,
or swing and swirl in the lab's blue light

like a feather caught and windblown?
Now, here you are blue-eyed and blinking,
chirping and gurgling, a raspberry
stuck on your thumb like a cap.

You find the berry, find your thumb,
find delight as the berry tumbles
into your baby-bird mouth. Your soul,
love, is held within you now,

even as I hold you on my lap.

Abide

Tho' much is taken, much abides.
> —Alfred, Lord Tennyson

Words were brimming from the patient's dark eyes,
his mouth was sewn into silence, barbed wire
of sutures crisscrossed the stubbled landscape
of what remained, his mouth now barricaded,
his jawline gone, crater after the bomb.

Beside him in the next bed, another kind
of war was being waged. Rage swarmed the mind
of this patient, the demons of DTs
now in command, biting, spitting, hitting
any enemy, and the enemy was me.

Only a thin, beige drape divided the men.
A border crossing between two nations,
I travelled from silence to chaos and
back again, unable to apprehend
the native tongue of either one, at last

speaking my own: *You must not hit the nurse.*
Suddenly from the man consigned to silence,
a clanging peal of bedrails. I assumed
the reality of cancer, of fresh wound,
of muteness, of endlessness of anguish,

was finally crushing down, about to drown
the man. Instead I was met by the sound
of his fist, marled and brown, punching his palm,
air cracking with each smack, until he calmed
enough to jab an accusing finger

toward the other man. He grasped my hand
in his own, liver-speckled and still strong,
defending me the only way he could,
and at last I was fluent in his language
of sorrow, of dignity, of flesh made word.

The Things We Ask

Of all of the things she could have asked—
for a sip of water, for another pain pill,
for a reason why her transplant failed,
the yellow woman lying in her bed
asked only if I could pray for her.

What could I say? The unsayable now
passed between us, a newborn absence,
a knowledge of her impending end
leaving us both untethered, beyond reason,
astronauts forgotten, left behind by their ship.

United in this outer space, we began
to pray, cold words sparking into flames
of despair, of hope, the way a meteor
descending ignites in the atmosphere,
unearthly light widening the sky for miles.

Chimera

I wonder some days if my donor was a dancer,
she said, gazing past me toward the exam room door.
I was removing her staples, delicately
crimping each one to form an *M*, the shape
of birds I drew in flocks as a child.
The seam of her wound a simple chevron,

a stranger's liver sewn beneath her ribs.
The staples slipped out easily, though her skin
was already growing around them,
her body so eager to embrace, to take in
something as foreign as surgical steel.
Was it really so impossible, then, her sense
of how a whole other person's life might feel?

Meridian

It's one of those things you can't see
or measure, but you know it's there,
insisted the Chinese doctor.

I knew exactly what he meant—
I could say the same thing about love
or madness or thoughts of rain.

He pointed to a map on the wall—
it could have been a map of the New York subway,
or the circuitry diagram for a microchip,

except that all the lines ran over a human form,
and the lines ran along points with poems for names,
like "Little Marsh" and "Spirit Door" and "Listening Palace."

It makes sense that you are having pain,
he said, as he placed the needle into the cool skin
on the top of my left foot, then placed another

above the fourth toenail of my left foot. *This one*
is called "Extreme Yin," he said, *good for your headaches*
and sleeping problems and also for dreams of ghosts.

I wondered how he knew
that only two nights before, my friend who died last spring
appeared for a second, beautiful and laughing,
then vanished again into my dream.

Birdwatching in Quarantine

The first days brought a Cooper's hawk, wings covering
her chicks high in the neighbor's hackberry
tree, her countenance unsparing as a death
sentence as she surveyed the treed canopy.

And as days turned to weeks, the scarlet flame
that burns on the head of the yellowhammer
appeared again and again, pentecost
daily descending upon the tulip poplar.

And purple finches and goldfinches flew
in two-by-two, male and female they came,
followed by the blur of the summer's first
ruby throat, humming despite our dismay.

On the fortieth day, rose-breasted grosbeaks—
a trio of them—took charge of the altar bearing
the birdseed and devoured the offered feast,
a kind of eucharist, at least for feathered things.

Grackle

An oil-slick of a bird,
midnight sheen in flight,
a blackened rainbow
plodding through the weeds
at the road's shoulder,
scavenging dead ants and stale fries—
you stop to stare at me,
take inventory with your
unapologetic amber eyes.
You find me wanting
and tilt your head at me,
pitying my blindness
to the feast right
in front of me.

Hawaiian Monk Seal

Do you remember the color of amber?
The sunlight angling toward September
transforms my fur to gold as I lumber
ashore to sleep along the ocean's border.

You have tagged me and numbered me.
I have become one of those things worthy
of being counted, finite as you. I see
you with one eye open as I wake briefly

between dreams of drifts of angelfish,
huge schools caught in swells and sluggish
to escape. I see you all, astonished
at my casual presence, brandishing

cameras in front of your faces like masks,
trying to save something long since passed.

Bittersweet Vine

Today, though November sews grey-brown seams
across the plains and white sky dulls the world,
the vine shows off bright red-orange berries
that gleam like jewels that have survived a war.

The cedar waxwings pluck them like greedy
children bobbing for apples, the flock of birds
consumed by winter's coming hungering,
and eating every sweet thing they can find.

I thought its only purpose was to curse
the earth. This twining vine that girdled oaks
and maples like razor wire sprung from dirt,
was one I'd pried loose, ripped up, cut down.

How many other living things have I scourged,
I wonder, thinking I was ordering my world?

Neglected Serapias

*The neglected Serapias, a rare orchid, has been found
in a Corsican military base in very large numbers:
more than 155,000 individuals!*
　　　　—ScienceDaily (February 25, 2022)

Here is a fracture, as fine a line
as a single newborn eyebrow.

Here is time like a jackhammer—
each minute, each second pounding

this old world harder than the last.
Together, like archeologists, they shape

a space, excavate and widen the gap
in the foundation of a gun turret

for something almost forgotten
to gain a foothold, curl roots in broken

concrete—a means of destruction
destroyed by an orchid's careless

flourishing, whose surfeit of purple,
speckled throats is silent as a choir

just before it sings Handel's chorus.

Found Coin

The coin has sorrow's face furrowed
on one side, kindness on the other—
I carry it with me now wherever I go.

Small and thinner than a dime,
I feel its crescent-moon curve
wedged in the crease of my right hip
as it rides in my jeans' front pocket.

Little hitchhiker, I picked it up
driving through Louisville, headed
back from Indiana, that flat land
like a page of prose, punctuated
with exclamations of grain silos.

It rode with me all the way.

When we stopped for gas,
the Amish man held the door for us
as we passed into the cool air,
smells of packs of peanuts, beef jerky,
the sweet tang of the Slurpee machine.

And the Amish girls nodded, white-capped
heads bowed even as they walked
through rows of pork rinds to the restroom,
no setting ever immune to reverence,

and the coin swayed in my pocket,
sorrow and kindness humming in time
with the thrum of the cooler in the back.

Julie Sumner is a poet who has worked as a critical care nurse, liver transplant coordinator, and massage therapist. She now teaches creative writing, focusing on reading poetry and writing as ways to develop resilience. She completed a Master of Fine Arts in poetry at Seattle Pacific University, a Master of Science in Nursing at Vanderbilt University, and a Bachelor of Arts in English at Birmingham-Southern College. Her work has appeared in *Delta Poetry Review*, *The Intima*, *Relief Journal*, *Wondrous Real*, *Catalpa Magazine*, and elsewhere.

This book is set in Optima typeface, developed by the German type-designer and calligrapher Hermann Zapf. Its inspiration came during Zapf's first trip to Italy in 1950. While in Florence he visited the cemetery of the Basilica di Santa Croce and was immediately taken by the design of the lettering found on the old tombstones there. He quickly sketched an early draft of the design on a 1000 lira banknote, and after returning to Frankfurt devoted himself to its development. It was first released as Optima by the D. Stempel AG foundry in 1958 and shortly thereafter by Mergenthaler in the United States. Inspired by classical Roman inscriptions and distinguished by its flared terminals, this typeface is prized for its curves and straights which vary minutely in thickness, providing a graceful and clear impression to the eye.